essentials

essentials provide up-to-date knowledge in a concentrated form. The essence of what matters as "state of the art" in the current professional discussion or in practice. essentials inform quickly, uncomplicatedly and comprehensibly

- as an introduction to a current topic from your field of expertise
- as an introduction to a subject area that is still unknown to you
- as an insight, in order to be able to speak on the subject

The books in electronic and printed form present the expert knowledge of Springer specialist authors in a compact form. They are particularly suitable for use as eBooks on tablet PCs, eBook readers and smartphones. essentials: Knowledge modules from economics, social sciences and the humanities, from technology and the natural sciences, as well as from medicine, psychology and the health professions. From renowned authors of all Springer publishing brands.

Phil C. Langer
Adina Dymczyk · Alina Brehm
Joram Ronel

Trauma concepts in research and practice

An Overview

 Springer

Phil C. Langer
Sozialpsychologie
International Psychoanalytic University
Berlin, Germany

Adina Dymczyk
Institut für Europäische Ethnologie
Humboldt-Universität zu Berlin
Berlin, Germany

Alina Brehm
Institut für Bildungswissenschaft
Universität Wien
Wien, Austria

Joram Ronel
Department für Psychosomatische
Medizin und Psychotherapie
Klinik Barmelweid
Barmelweid, Switzerland

ISSN 2197-6708   ISSN 2197-6716   (electronic)
essentials
ISBN 978-3-658-40483-3   ISBN 978-3-658-40484-0   (eBook)
https://doi.org/10.1007/978-3-658-40484-0

This Springer imprint is published by the registered company Springer Fachmedien Wiesbaden GmbH, part of Springer Nature.
The registered company address is: Abraham-Lincoln-Str. 46, 65189 Wiesbaden, Germany

What You Can Find in This *Essential*

- A historical outline of the development of the trauma discourse
- An overview of different – clinical, psychosocial, transgenerational and collective – concepts of trauma, their theoretical and empirical foundations
- Examples of the application of these concepts in selected – therapeutic, institutional, research and sociopolitical – fields of practice
- A critical reflection on key conceptual challenges
- Suggestions for productive appropriations of the concepts in one's own work with trauma

Contents

Introduction

Trauma is a sign of our time. "The globalized dimensions of war, torture, genocide, natural and famine catastrophes with a mass migration that has now also reached European states for several years" have contributed, according to Hans-Peter Kapfhammer (2018), "to the fact that traumatic events and their health consequences are given central attention in the public consciousness". This is supported by the increasing socio-political awareness of traumatic experiences of sexualised and racist violence. Trauma is not only discussed in psychology and medicine. The term is referred to in debates in sociology, political science, literature and cultural studies, and it has also entered media discourse and everyday language: The school gym seems to evoke traumatic memories, everyone has a "maths trauma" and the traumas of cancelled holiday flights are exchanged in internet forums. A *Google search* for "trauma" currently yields about 300 million hits, and over 4 million results appear on *Google Scholar*. It is likely that references will grow significantly over the next few years as we attempt to process the collective experience of the COVID-19 pandemic. One might almost ask: Is everything trauma or what?

But when we say "trauma" are we actually talking about the same thing? In a psychological sense alone, different understandings of trauma are at play when prevalences of trauma sequelae after a tsunami are measured as a *natural disaster*, when the profound destruction of social trust among victims of political persecution is attempted to be understood as a *human-made disaster* via a psychosocial conception of trauma, when dynamics of the transmission of trauma across generations in families of survivors of the Shoah are examined, and when experiences of racial violence in the USA are conceived in terms of a collective historical trauma. All of this is somehow related to violence and the consequences it produces. The Greek word *trauma* (τραύμα) translates as "wound," that is, an injury caused by

P. C. Langer et al., *Trauma concepts in research and practice*, essentials, https://doi.org/10.1007/978-3-658-40484-0_1

exposure to violence. The metaphorical use in the sense of psychological trauma is evident in the talk of "wounds of the soul." It signifies a subjective condition of being overwhelmed, the impossibility of "adequately" processing the experiences of violence one is confronted with, which may not even have to have been experienced by oneself, individually, in concrete social relations or as an imagined collective. This is rather vague, but the commonality of meaning of the different conceptions of trauma does not go much further. Misunderstandings are thus inherent and sometimes deliberately provoked, even sharp struggles for interpretive authority as to which understanding of trauma is the "correct" one can be observed.

The aim of our book is to try to provide a little orientation in this confusion, to contribute to a reflected use of the concept of trauma in research and practice, and to open up a discursive space for productive exchange. After giving a brief history of trauma discourse in Chap. 2, in the following chapters we introduce the most important concepts of trauma, illustrate their use in practice by means of case studies, and discuss contextual strengths and limitations of the scientific and practical reference to trauma: in a clinical sense (Chap. 3), in a psychosocial understanding (Chap. 4), in the form of transgenerational transmission (Chap. 5), and as a collective phenomenon (Chap. 6). Finally, we outline considerations for the future of trauma discourse (Chap. 7).

This book is, of course, highly ambivalent in itself: it is intended to provide orientation in the face of a discursive conjuncture of which it is at the same time a part. It should present the different concepts neutrally and on an equal footing in a field that is highly politicized in the struggle for interpretive authority, whereby precisely the claim to neutrality itself becomes a political issue. Where we have succeeded, sometimes well, sometimes less well, and perhaps sometimes not at all, in translating these ambivalences into insightful reading experiences is ultimately for you, the reader, to decide. To the extent that the book draws on our many years of work in various trauma-related fields of teaching, research and practice, it is itself an expression of processes of negotiation that are not always easy but, we believe, rewarding.

A Brief History of Trauma Discourse

2

The term trauma has its origins in accident medicine. Since the nineteenth century, the psychological concept of trauma has developed from models of traumatic neurosis with the assumption that mental traumatization can have a pathogenic effect (Sect. 2.1). In the context of the two world wars, the reference to trauma can be understood as a struggle for recognition of the experience of injustice (Sect. 2.2). The introduction of post-traumatic stress disorder (PTSD) as a clinical diagnosis in 1980 indicates the current dominant paradigm in the history of trauma discourse (Sect. 2.3).

2.1 The Beginnings of Trauma Theory

The development of a scientific concept of trauma since the 1860s is closely linked to the consequences of modernization. With the expansion of railways, accidents occurred that brought with them discussions as to whether the victims would suffer from psychological as well as physical effects (Lehmacher 2013). **John Eric Erichsen** (1818–1896) attributed the consequences of trauma to spinal concussion during the collisions, the severity of which he linked to the terror suffered by those affected.

Jean-Martin Charcot (1825–1893) also developed the theory of traumatic hysteria in the late nineteenth century. He observed that people were affected by certain ailments even without demonstrable physical damage and even after a certain latency period following the traumatic events. His theory of an "agent provocateur" enabled him to explain how external events acted on individuals in a

P. C. Langer et al., *Trauma concepts in research and practice*, essentials, https://doi.org/10.1007/978-3-658-40484-0_2

manner similar to that of a trigger and produced symptoms of hysteria; however, he also argued that there must be a predisposition in the individuals affected. It is due to the scientifically exact and anti-stigmatizing approach of Charcot, who influenced many neurologists of his time, that the concept of a post-traumatic syndrome has found its way into contemporary medical thinking.

Hermann Oppenheim (1858–1919) introduced the term traumatic neurosis in 1889 and initially located its cause in the brain. He saw a disposition of the nervous system as the reason why some people showed stronger "disorders" than others (Schmiedebach 2019). Controversy arose within the medical profession as to whether the symptoms could be faked. Disparagingly, people spoke of the onset of "retirement neurosis" as a consequence.

Sigmund Freud (1856–1939) developed a psychodynamic theory that defined the onset of neurosis as a *subsequently* experienced trauma. He initially saw the emergence of neuroses as a result of sexual abuse in children. According to this theory, the cause lay in an environment marked by violence and concrete events. Later he distanced himself from his "seduction theory" and located the reason for traumatic neuroses in the processing of early childhood experiences in adulthood, which was conceived as *"afterwardsness"*. He also saw the subsequent embedding of potentially traumatic experiences as decisive for the development of other traumas, such as those of soldiers in the First World War.

Pierre Janet (1859–1947) viewed trauma as a reaction to an event that occurred in childhood. He argued that hysteria must have its origin in psychological trauma. His thesis of dissociation as a consequence of an overwhelming affective experience, which causes a loss of the integrating function of consciousness, is still the core of post-traumatic theory today.

With the First World War and the soldiers freed from frontline operations as "war tremors", the dispute about possible simulation was reignited. Was it a traumatic neurosis or hysteria? Various theories of war neurosis, shock neurosis, shellshock, war hysteria, trench neurosis were drafted to try to understand the phenomenon. While Oppenheim felt his theory was validated, the diagnosis of "traumatic neurosis" was only reluctantly assigned (Lehmacher 2013, p. 42). The theory of hysteria, on the other hand, experienced a resurgence. It diverted attention from a connection between war experiences and following consequences for soldiers. Thus, the theory of hysteria regained popularity in the logic of those treating them, whose main concern was to avoid further economic damage of the state through an "epidemic of pension neurosis" (ibid.). In order to send the supposedly war-refusing soldiers back to the front, some doctors sometimes applied cruel measures such as electric shocks (which is still the custom under certain conditions).

At the same time, modern psychoanalytic psychosomatic medicine emerged from treatment experiences with these "war tremblers" and was able to establish treatment standards that are still valid today, including group therapy principles.

2.2   A Paradigmatic Extension

The American stress researcher **Walter Cannon** (1871–1945) approached the phenomenon of trauma-associated disorders from a physiological perspective. Cannon, a biologist and physician who coined the *fight-or-flight theory*, was also concerned as a military doctor in World War I with the effects of psychological trauma on physical processes, e.g. on wound healing in injured soldiers. His findings can be seen as pioneering precursors for psychoneuroimmunological connections of current concepts and underline the biological character of trauma-related disorders.

Between the world wars, interest in trauma theories initially ebbed. It was not until the consequences of the Second World War became apparent that trauma research picked up again. **Abram Kardiner** (1891–1981) is considered a pioneer in the development of PTSD with his work The *Traumatic Neuroses of War*, which received considerable attention immediately before the United States entered World War II and systematically presented the symptomatology of war neuroses (Young 1995, p. 89). In contrast to Freud, who was concerned with trauma primarily in terms of defense mechanisms, Kardiner explained neurosis as a process of adaptation to the changing environment. According to him, traumatic experience led to an overstimulation of the person, who was too overwhelmed to react to the environment and experienced this as a loss of control. Kardiner's teaching fell into oblivion; it was only with the introduction of the concept of PTSD that it was received again.

According to Didier Fassin and Richard Rechtman (2009), the aftermath of World War II represented a twofold paradigm shift associated with particularly extreme experiences of violence and the long period of silence following the event: "It is because of the delay between the event and its painful exposure to the public gaze that the process can be qualified as trauma" (ibid., p. 18). The consequences of National Socialism also played a central role in the development of the trauma discourse in German politics (Laub 2005). The reaction of the Federal Republic can be briefly described as a policy of refusing to pay out compensation and to acknowledge suffering, which was characterized by anti-Semitically motivated ascriptions of guilt against Jewish claimants, while at the same time the so-called "denazification victims" in the non-Jewish population were readily granted pension claims. Psychiatric experts often attributed the psychological consequences of genocidal persecution more to the "condition" of the plaintiffs than to the National Socialist crimes (Herzog 2017, p. 98). Israeli and American psychiatrists and psychoanalysts used counter-assessments to advocate for the victims. They wanted to prove that the survivors suffered from symptoms that could be traced back to concentration camp imprisonment. They summarized these symptoms as *survivor syndromes*. The peculiarity of the term "survivor syndrome" lies in the fact that the experience of being affected is linked with strength and the idea of witnessing.

To this day, trauma discourse is closely linked to the struggle for recognition of experiencing injustice – not only with regard to monetary compensation. This situation results in a central tension: the political recognition of injustice can lead to the pathologization of a group on the basis of its experience. The consequences of genocidal persecution shape societies and encourage us to view trauma in the context of political processes.

2.3   PTSD: Discovery or Invention?

The emergence of the concept of PTSD in the USA in the 1970s was linked to the sociopolitical reappraisal of the Vietnam War. The "crazy Vietnam vet" – alcoholic, violent, suicidal – became a well-known figure in the media. **Robert Lifton** (*1926) devoted himself to it in the book *Home from the War.* In this book, he criticized the efforts of psychiatrists to achieve quick successes in the treatment of war veterans so that they could soon be sent back to the front, and pleaded for diagnostic recognition of their suffering as a separate mental disorder. The *Diagnostic and Statistical Manual of Mental Disorders* (DSM-III) of the *American Psychiatric Association* (APA) finally introduced the diagnosis *Post Traumatic Stress Disorder* (PTSD) in 1980. In 1991, the diagnosis was included in the *International Classification of Diseases* (ICD-10) of the World Health Organization (WHO). Paradoxically, the diagnosis of PTSD entailed a depoliticization: through the psychological focus on the causality of event and symptomatology, political processes were largely ignored.

PTSD is – depending on one's perspective – an "invention" or "discovery" of the 1970s. Young (1995, p. 5) describes its emergence as a phenomenon "glued together by the practices, technologies, and narratives with which it is diagnosed, studied, treated, and represented and by the various interests, institutions, and moral arguments that mobilized these efforts and resources". Today, an inflationary use of the term is often problematized, which makes it all the more important to talk about experiences of "suffering, shock, pain, loss, and mourning" (Brunner 2014, p. 16) without subsuming everything under PTSD and trauma.

The Clinical Concept of Trauma

3

In this chapter, we present the clinical understanding of trauma with a focus on post-traumatic stress disorder. After outlining selected basic principles (Sect. 3.1), we provide a current practical example in the form of the institutionalization of treatment options to PTSD in the German armed forces (Sect. 3.2) and open up critical perspectives on clinical understanding (Sect. 3.3).

3.1 Theoretical Foundations and Empirical Findings

The experience of an extreme event that lead to sustained overburdening of psychological processing abilities is the starting point of the clinical understanding of trauma: no trauma without a traumatic event. In this sense, the ICD-10 refers to short- or long-lasting events or occurrences "of extraordinary threat or catastrophic magnitude that would cause profound distress in almost anyone" (WHO 1994, p. 344). Somewhat more specifically, the DSM-5 refers to an event or events that involve a confrontation with "actual or threatened death, serious injury, or sexual violence" (APA 2013, p. 271).[1]

The types of traumatic events can be differentiated in two ways: First, they can be experienced once or short-term (so-called type I traumas) or repeatedly or

---

[1] This is understood as direct experience, personal witnessing by another person, communication of the experience by a family member or close friend, or confrontation in a repetitive manner with aversive details of a traumatic situation.

© The Author(s), under exclusive license to Springer Fachmedien Wiesbaden GmbH, part of Springer Nature 2023
P. C. Langer et al., *Trauma concepts in research and practice*, essentials, https://doi.org/10.1007/978-3-658-40484-0_3

long-term (type II traumas).[2] Secondly, they can be (more or less) accidental – this applies in particular to so-called *natural disasters* – or they can be of an interpersonal nature – so-called *human-made disasters*.

Traumatic events are necessary but not sufficient conditions for the development of trauma-related disorders such as PTSD: Not every traumatic event results in a trauma in the clinical sense. *Human-made disasters* in particular have a significantly higher potential for the development of PTSD.

Research examining the prevalence of PTSD criteria among survivors of the Shoah found high prevalence rates of between 40% and 74% (Kuch and Cox 1992; Trappler et al. 2002). It was striking that many survivors nevertheless developed an astonishing degree of "normality" and functionality over decades, which usually said little about the survivors' inner and relational world (Ronel 2020).

Maercker (2013) proposed a multifactorial framework and modulation model that includes five etiological factor groups: pretraumatic risk or protective factors, peritraumatic event factors, posttraumatic maintenance factors, posttraumatic resources and health promoting factors, as well as posttraumatic processes and outcomes (see Fig. 3.1).

Of course the severity of the trauma itself plays an important role in the manifestation of PTSD, but it is also significantly influenced by the way a person evaluates the event. Maercker (2013, p. 38) notes: "If the trauma victim is able to see a margin of influence – however small – during the traumatic event, the posttraumatic consequences will usually not be so pronounced." In terms of maintaining factors, post-traumatic life stresses – such as separations or inability to work – were among the major factors in the existence of chronic stress disorders. The experience of trauma can profoundly alter the subject's relationship to the self and the social environment. Feelings such as guilt (having survived), shame, anger and revenge can be essential in maintaining the post-traumatic situation.

How can we understand post-traumatic processes? According to Janet, dissociations can be understood as the consequence of an overwhelming affective experience that causes a loss of the integrating function of consciousness. These persist partly unnoticed or unconsciously and can be experienced as images, nightmares, fantasies, or embodiment, and can often be reenacted in behavior (Eckhardt-Henn and Spitzer 2018). In addition to the formation of dissociations as an attempted solution – according to object relations theory – introspections of malignant perpetrators often develop in the sense of a psychological "emergency mechanism", particularly in the case of relationship-related repetitive traumatisation, when a

---

[2] It is under discussion to what extent medically induced traumas, for example due to life-threatening illness, should supplement this classification.

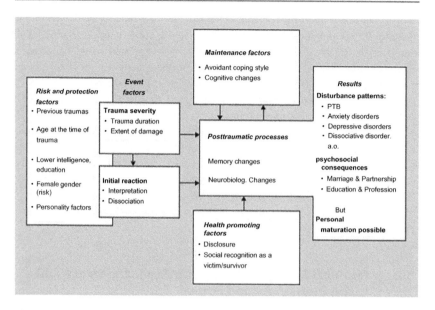

Fig. 3.1 Framework model of the etiology of trauma-related disorders. (Maercker 2013, p. 37)

fight-or-flight response is not possible and only withdrawal inwards seems to be the only option. The organism tries to protect itself by means of introjection and identification with the aggressor and thus to integrate the experienced traumatization in this dysfunctional way. The economy of the development of a trauma disorder therefore always depends on the "unbearable outside" versus salutogenetically relevant inner-psychic processing. Specific, partly malignant countertransferences and the danger of entanglement in the psychotherapeutic work with PTSD patients result from this. Supervision and a high capacity of self-reflection therefore becomes necessary for diagnostic understanding.

Central to clinical understanding – especially with regard to diagnostics and related therapeutic practice – is the unfolding of the disorder pattern of PTSD by specifying its defining symptoms. PTSD is mostly characterized by three symptom complexes: intrusive memories of the trauma (e.g. flashbacks), systematic avoidance of circumstances resembling or related to the stress, and physical and cognitive symptoms of hyperactivity (autonomic hyperarousal). It is noteworthy that there are clear differences between the classification systems and between their individual versions. The ICD-10 is close to this tripartite structure, but the ICD 11, which will come into effect in 2023, has announced reduction of the symptoms defining PTSD and at the same time a distinction is made between classic PTSD and complex PTSD (C-PTSD), the cause of which is primarily understood to be interpersonal traumatic events and for which further diagnostic requirements are made beyond PTSD (Brewin 2020; Elliott et al. 2021). Compared to the DSM-IV, the tripartite symptom structure was abandoned for the DSM-5 in favor of a 4-dimensional model. Four symptom clusters now list 20 individual symptoms.

These differences, which remind us that they are contested discursive constructions, are not trivial. The resulting challenges for diagnosis and therapy can have political significance. It makes a difference, for example, whether war- and flight-related trauma is diagnosed in asylum procedures using ICD-10/11 or DSM-5 (Dreßing 2016). In a study on childhood sexual abuse, Hyland et al. (2016) found that 60% of adult participants met the DSM-5 criteria for PTSD, but only 49% met the ICD-11 criteria.

3.2   Practical Example: The Institutionalization of PTSD in the German Armed Forces

From a sociopolitical perspective, it would have been obvious to address the role of PTSD in the context of work with refugees or to trace the ambivalences of this diagnosis in relation to victims of sexualized or racist violence, which, in addition to important therapeutic possibilities, is also inherent in the danger of depoliticizing the psychopathologization of social problems (e.g. Gerdau et al. 2017; Keupp et al. 2016; Pole et al. 2005; Streeck-Fischer 2019). However, we have chosen to look at the institutionalization of PTSD in the German Armed Forces ("Bundeswehr") as a practical example, as it is a good way to show how a powerful trauma disposition emerged in just a few years that is socially and politically consequential.

The foundation of the Psychotrauma Centre of the Bundeswehr in Berlin in 2010 goes back to a cross-faction motion in the German Bundestag. In this motion, the Federal Government was called upon to bring together existing and new facilities for the psychosocial treatment and care of PTSD sufferers in a "knowledge and research centre" on an empirical basis. The background to this was the development of the Bundeswehr's area of responsibility. With the deployment in Afghanistan as part of the ISAF mission, German soldiers were confronted with hitherto unfamiliar dangers and a high intensity of violence (Seiffert et al. 2011). In addition to the "normal" challenges of foreign missions, such as separation from friends and family, there were rocket attacks and explosive traps.

The number of soldiers diagnosed with psychological problems in the context of foreign deployments has increased significantly since the mid-2000s. Reports of experiences were published (e.g. Wizelman 2009), self-help networks were founded, and the pressure to act in order to address deployment-related stresses both preventively and therapeutically grew. Part of the problem was that psychological problems in military contexts go hand in hand with a high potential of stigma. The (self-)image of soldiers (especially on deployment) is one of strength. This applies not least to notions of heroic masculinity. In this respect, it is not surprising that fear of stigmatization, career disadvantages, and loss of reputation among comrades and superiors are among the most frequently cited reasons that prevent soldiers from seeking help for psychological problems (Hoge et al. 2004).

In the spirit of the scientific investigation demanded by the Bundestag, Wittchen and colleagues (2012) conducted a dark field study with soldiers after their deployment to Afghanistan. Almost half of them reported a traumatic experience. Twelve months after their return, 3% of the study participants had developed a PTSD diagnosis, whereby, as expected, those soldiers who were stationed in violent locations were overrepresented. Since then, numerous empirical studies have been conducted within the framework of the Psychotrauma Centre, which have influenced the discourse on PTSD in the Bundeswehr beyond its therapeutic benefits (e.g. Schuy et al. 2019 on the stigma of mental illness).

In addition to scientific research, the focus of the Psychotrauma Center is on the prevention and treatment of the psychological aftermath of deployment. With the focus on mission-related stress, the field of activity of military psychology has changed significantly since the end of the Cold War. The focus on PTSD has also had far-reaching institutional consequences in the Bundeswehr: Thus, handouts on dealing with PTSD for superiors, training and further education concepts, assistance for affected soldiers and relatives and – in cooperation with the Protestant Church – a children's book are available. Within less than ten years, the diagnosis of PTSD as an institutional thematic pathway has made it possible to turn psychological vulnerability from a highly stigmatized "no go" topic into a sensitized and caring approach for soldiers with deployment experience.

The reference to PTSD and the associated therapy and support options are undoubtedly vital for many soldiers. The delegation of the topic to a special institution is problematic, however, as the difficult and unprocessed experiences from deployment are thus marked as an individual and psychopathologically relevant problem for which expert help is available. In this way, the socio-political relevance of the topic recedes into the background, the experiences of violence brought into society by the soldiers are "contained", kept latent, and do not have to be discussed further in public (Langer 2013). It therefore seems important to complement the institutionalization of PTSD in the Bundeswehr with a discourse in society as a whole on experiences of and dealing with violence during deployment.

3.3   Critical Reflection

Diagnoses always reflect the contemporary epoch and culture in which they are defined. Edward Shorter (1993), a medical historian who has studied the history of psychosomatic illness, speaks of the phenomenon of "pathoplasticity" in this context. The concept is used to describe the mutability of the social legitimation of illness over time, but also of the specific environment. Social perceptions of diseases change.

The explicit eminence-based (as opposed to evidence-based) nature of diagnostic catalogues such as the ICD or DSM contradicts a natural science approach of a primarily atheoretical approach (Traicu and Joober 2017). Although not consistently validated, often mutually overlapping, and unclearly delineated, the now established disorder groups have proven clinically useful. A diagnostic consensus has been reached over the development of the last decades.

In everyday clinical practice, medical reports are formulated with an often lengthy list of different acute psychopathological diagnoses. For example, the diagnosis of an affective, an anxiety, a functional/somatoform and a post-traumatic disorder can be found in the same patient during the same treatment. The graphical representations of such results are impressive (cf. Fig. 3.2), as the multidimensionality of the constructs is striking. The diagnostic partialization, thus, appears as a helpless concretistic implementation of these diagnostic systems, while a fundamental concept of disease and health is often lacking.

Critical objections also recognize in the clinical understanding of trauma:

- Psychopathologizing: What does it mean to diagnose a mental disorder as PTSD, which after all could also be understood as a "normal" (or even "healthy") reaction to an "abnormal" (or "pathological") situation (war, torture, abuse)?
- Individualization: Is the diagnosis understood only as individual suffering, leaving aside the fact that the violence that takes place in the traumatic event is in many cases (war-related violence, sexualized or racist violence) a social one, i.e. it is a collectively related suffering? Does this mean that the political dimension of the articulation and recognition of social experiences of suffering is lost?

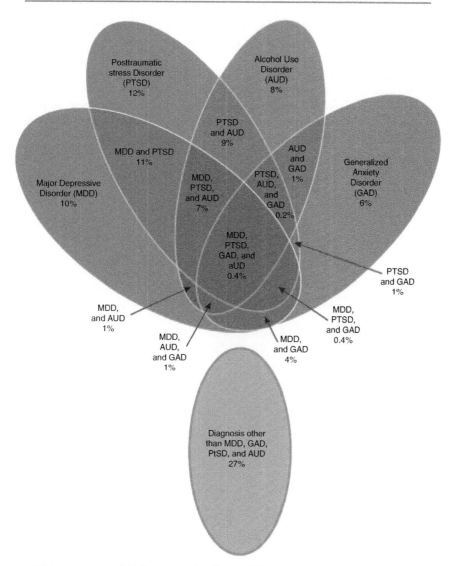

^a Rates are average weighted percentages from Houston VA/Menninger (N=264).

Fig. 3.2 Representation of comorbidity correlations. (Regier et al. 2013)

- Assumption of normality: Doesn't the "post" in PTSD refer to a state after traumatisation, which in many cases – in ongoing conflict contexts – simply does not exist?
- Indifference to the nature of the traumatic event: Is there not a striking difference between *natural* and *human-made disasters* in terms of consequences? Could it not be said that in the case of natural disasters something terrible happens outside in the world, while in the case of the other kind the social world itself and trust in it is destroyed?

Psychosocial Understandings of Trauma

4

In this chapter we broaden the view from a symptom-oriented clinical understanding to the social and political contexts that reveal trauma as a psychosocial process. The presentation of different conceptions (Sect. 4.1) is followed by a practical example from research with child soldiers (Sect. 4.2), before we point out conceptual blurring (Sect. 4.3).

4.1   Theoretical Foundations and Empirical Findings

Psychosocial views refer to a common basic understanding of trauma as a socially mediated process. In this sense, the concept of trauma is always already political and makes it possible to articulate experiences of suffering from social conditions of violence.

Ariane Brenssell (2014, p. 123) vividly describes the shaping of her view of trauma through her work with women who have experienced sexualised violence:

> Trauma […] is something individual and social, something political and personal at the same time. Rape is a fundamental shock, something incomprehensible, an experience of disempowerment and powerlessness – inflicted by another human being – with far-reaching consequences for those affected. Social prejudices and taboos are attached to rape.

Becker (2014, p. 26) begins his book *The Invention of Trauma* with a reflection on his own psychotherapeutic experiences with extremely traumatized victims of persecution and torture by Pinochet's dictatorial military regime in Chile:

© The Author(s), under exclusive license to Springer Fachmedien
Wiesbaden GmbH, part of Springer Nature 2023
P. C. Langer et al., *Trauma concepts in research and practice*, essentials,
https://doi.org/10.1007/978-3-658-40484-0_4

Psychological suffering can never be understood and treated independently of the social context. This is especially true in a totalitarian system such as the Chilean dictatorship. Only through a conscious reflection of the social context can the complicated dialectic between individual suffering and extreme socio-political processes be grasped.

The political dimension of trauma is not least evident in genocidal violence (Langer and Brehm 2020). Psychosocial approaches to trauma focus on *human-made disasters* as violent conditions produced by human beings.

The concept of psychosocial trauma goes back to **Ignacio Martín-Baró**, a founder of liberation psychology in the context of the civil war in El Salvador. Liberation psychology aims at "the development of critical consciousness […] as well as the empowerment of people so that they can free themselves from oppression and socially unjust structures" (Schroer-Hippel et al. 2018, p. 101). Baró describes trauma as a "crystallization of social abhorrent and dehumanized relationships" formed in individuals (cited in Repnik 2018, p. 32):

> By speaking of psychosocial trauma, one insists that trauma has been socially produced and therefore its understanding and resolution lies not only in addressing the individual's problem, but its social roots, that is, the social traumatogenic structures and conditions. (ibid.)

Bruno Bettelheim already presented fundamental considerations for a psychosocial understanding of trauma. As an Austrian Jew, Bettelheim was imprisoned in Nazi concentration camps at the end of the 1930s. He analysed his experiences in 1943 in the essay *Individual and Mass Behavior in Extreme Situations*. According to him, we find ourselves in an extreme situation

> […] when we are catapulted into a situation where our old adaptive mechanisms and values no longer help, and where even some of them endanger our lives instead of protecting them as before. In this situation we are, so to speak, deprived of our entire defence system, and we are thrown back so far that we have to develop – according to the situation – new attitudes, ways of life and values. (Bettelheim 1980, p. 20)

An extreme situation, the psychological correlate of which appears to be extreme traumatization, is characterized by "the inevitability of a life situation of imprisonment, its uncertain duration and the permanent threat to survival" (Bogner and Rosenthal 2019, p. 38), as well as the loss of trust in one's fellow social world. What does this mean for the possibility of processing trauma? Bettelheim refers to feelings of shame and guilt associated with survival, as well as feelings of immediacy and speechlessness.

Also in relation to the Shoah, **Hans Keilson** (1992) developed his concept of sequential traumatization, which has inspired many current conceptualizations of trauma in psychosocial terms. In a study of Jewish orphans who survived the German occupation of the Netherlands and the Nazi extermination, he differentiated three traumatic sequences: (1) the enemy occupation of the Netherlands with incipient terror against the Jewish minority; (2) direct persecution, deportation and confinement in concentration camps, hiding in improvised wartime foster families; and (3) the postwar period, marked by the debate whether the children should remain in Dutch families or be placed in a Jewish environment. Talk of trauma as a process becomes immediately apparent here: it is not the one, singular violent event that describes trauma, but the longer-term course of events with a complex interweaving of different traumatic sequences. Keilson's study drew attention to the fact that it was not so much the second sequence of persecution, which was to be assessed most intensively in terms of experienced violence, but the third sequence, that of the post-war period, which was essential for the outcome and the final assessment of the massive-cumulative traumatisation event.

Becker (2014) has made Keilson's concept fruitful for a critical understanding of traumatizing processes in the context of migration and flight. In this respect, Fig. 4.1 illustrates a psychosocial trauma process in the context of seeking asylum, whereby phases 3 and 4, which are situated in a host country after flight, are

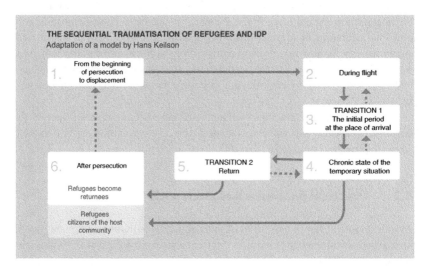

Fig. 4.1 Model of sequential traumatisation in the context of forced migration and flight. (GIZ 2019, p. 20)

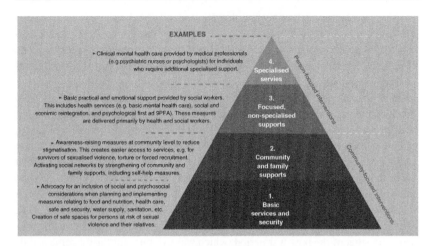

Fig. 4.2 Intervention pyramid for psychosocial support in conflict areas. (GIZ 2019, p. 25)

also essential, as they are often accompanied by existential experiences of insecurity and processing the migratory experiences hardly seems possible.

In practice, psychosocial understandings of trauma go hand in hand with interdisciplinary and multiprofessional approaches to intervention. This is expressed in the intervention pyramid (see Fig. 4.2), which is used as a benchmark in international humanitarian and development cooperation. It builds on psychosocial work, emphasises the importance of communities, for example in terms of destigmatising mental illness, and points to the need to take psychosocial aspects into account at all levels, for example by creating safe spaces for people who have been victims of sexualised violence.

Psychosocial understandings of trauma are linked to an ethical stance in that they call for taking sides and abandoning the precept of neutrality taught in therapeutic approaches (Becker 2014, p. 46).

4.2   Practical Example: Research with Child Soldiers

As an example of how a psychosocial understanding of trauma can guide psychological and social science practice, we present a research project with former child soldiers of the 'Islamic State' (ISIS) in northern Iraq, conducted in 2018 and 2019 (Langer and Ahmad 2019). The aim of the project was to identify children's psychosocial needs in order to improve or develop support services. In the tradition of participatory action research, the project aimed to strengthen children's social agency through research-based intervention.

Child soldiers played an important role in the ideological system of the terrorist organization as the future generation of the caliphate, as easily formed fighters and as (also sexual) service providers, and were systematically and often violently recruited, ideologically indoctrinated and militarily drilled. Many were involved in battles and attacks. After their liberation, they were often detained by Iraqi or Kurdish security agencies, interrogated, sometimes using torture, imprisoned or placed in camps where they were not allowed to reveal their past lest they suffer reprisals or violence. In political and social perception, they were considered perpetrators and were highly stigmatized. The experiences of child soldiers, in which perpetrator and victim components are intertwined, can best be captured by the concept of extreme traumatisation. They go beyond what can be described by the clinical diagnosis of PTSD. The understanding of sequential traumatization allows for the perspective that not only the time in ISIS, but also after ISIS as an essential phase of processing the traumatic experiences. It is noteworthy that little is known to date about what is therapeutically effective in working with child soldiers. The few published studies do not convey any viable results that point beyond the specific contexts and group.

In order to answer the question of what the children deployed by ISIS as soldiers in northern Iraq experienced, what condition they were in after liberation, and what they would need in order to achieve a minimum of psychological integrity and social agency, the method of collaborative storytelling was developed for the study. The idea was to form small groups of three to five children who had been affiliated with ISIS and to initiate a process of collaboratively developing a story with a fictional ISIS child soldier as the protagonist. The story was to begin before the ISIS era, address access and experiences in the ISIS as well as exit from the ISIS and the current situation, and include an open perspective on the future. The following theoretical assumptions guided the development of the methodological approach and indicate a way of transferring a psychosocial understanding of trauma into the practice of research as an intervention:

- The importance of narratives has been widely noted in trauma-related research and therapy. Through the coherent and meaningful stories developed, children are able to distance themselves from the difficult past and integrate the experiences into their biographical identity narratives.
- As the group develops a fictional story, an "as if" mode comes into play, which is also used in psychotherapeutic approaches. It makes it possible to express one's own story in the name of the fictional character. Especially in shame-ridden,

stigmatized contexts of articulation, this seems helpful. Particularly in institutionally highly controlled settings such as prison, telling the "real" story would be potentially dangerous, which is why the possibility of fictionalization takes into account the research ethical imperative of "do no harm".

- The joint development of a storyline includes a playful moment, which makes the approach particularly suitable for working with children. The risk of retraumatisation is also minimised.
- Collective narratives are, after all, an essential prerequisite for the articulation of individual traumatic experiences. We know this from research with survivors of the Shoah, who could only speak publicly about their lives once a cultural narrative about the Shoah was in place. Collaborative storytelling aimed to create a discourse space through diverse narratives that would allow other children to articulate their respective specific experiences.

The development of the stories was accompanied by a manual with guiding questions by regional field researchers who had already worked with former child soldiers in different settings and had built up a trusting relationship. The stories, generated over a period of several weeks and published as a booklet, helped to better understand the children's psychosocial needs (e.g., with regard to experiences of alienation and the meaning of guilt; see Langer 2020). However, the therapeutic benefits of the method in terms of improvement in psychological and psychosocial state could only be recorded subjectively in the project and need to be investigated more systematically in follow-up studies. The hope is that Collaborative Storytelling can prove to be a participatory method of psychosocial trauma work. Of course, it does not replace specific therapeutic work, but it creates a space in which this can begin in the first place.

4.3   Critical Reflection

"The modern Western view of trauma and its health consequences," writes Kapfhammer (2018), "has focused primarily on the dimension of individual suffering and largely omitted important sociocultural contexts. Human crises and catastrophes also increasingly became the exclusive province of medicine, especially psychiatry and psychotherapy." Psychosocial understandings of trauma respond to this critique by emphasizing the social mediation and political dimensions of violent relationships.

Critically, it is often unclear what is meant by psychosocial in each case. An example from peace and conflict research: Miller and Rasmussen (2010) argue for considering trauma-focused and psychosocial theoretical frameworks together. To do so, they use less of a processual understanding of trauma, but discuss everyday events as psychosocial stressors (to which they unsystematically include precarious poverty and unemployment, difficult housing and educational conditions, as well as traffic congestion, air pollution, and political insecurity) to mental health – which they make measurable with reference to PTSD. The conception thus remains ambivalent: it expands purely clinical notions of trauma by including contextual stress experiences, which in violent conflicts are always to be understood politically as well, and can thus be connected to the psychosocial understanding of trauma presented here, but adheres to a simplified causal effect model regarding stress theories, through which it can find resonance in conventional PTSD debates.

Transgenerational Transmission of Trauma

The understandings of trauma presented so far have been based on the assumption that an individual has experienced a traumatic event. In this chapter, we present approaches that explore the question of whether and how trauma is transmitted transgenerationally (Sect. 5.1). Using the example of a psychotherapeutic treatment of a Shoah survivor in the context of the destructive relationship dynamics with his son, we show symptoms and mechanisms of transmission (Sect. 5.2) before touching on critical aspects of the discussion (Sect. 5.3).

5.1 Theoretical Foundations and Empirical Findings

Transgenerational approaches capture the conscious or unconscious transmission of symptoms through interpersonal relationships *psychologically* and *psychodynamically*, the transmission of trauma within the family system through communication *systemically* and *communicatively*, the transmission of social norms and beliefs from one generation to the next *socioculturally*, as well as genetic and epigenetic aspects *biologically*.[1] In the following we present family systemic and psychodynamic models as well as an integrative multidimensional model.

Judith S. Kestenberg (1989) developed the term "time tunnel" and the concept of "transposition" based on her clinical work with children of Shoah survivors. Transposition describes the experience of children of survivors as if passing

---

[1] Biological mechanisms of transmission include genetic predispositions for inherited vulnerability to PTSD and epigenetic approaches (Yehuda et al. 2015; Roth Tania 2014; Franklin et al. 2010).

P. C. Langer et al., *Trauma concepts in research and practice*, essentials, https://doi.org/10.1007/978-3-658-40484-0_5

through a tunnel into the time of their parents' persecution and living simultaneously in the present and the past. Their parents' traumatic past becomes a part of their own present reality. In this, the relatives murdered in the Shoah, whom the children never knew but who are tangibly present for them in parental mourning, take on an important role. The identification with the often depressed parents can lead the children to the unconscious experience that the parents are dead and can only be revived if the lost objects can be brought back. Kestenberg describes that the depressive and anxiety-producing feelings of the children become somatized when they descend into the tunnel, that is, they find expression in physical symptoms. The nature of these symptoms is already determined by the type of parental interaction during bodily care in early childhood, in which the survivors pass on physically traumatic experiences to the children who thus make their first contact with the time tunnel.

Haydée Faimberg (1988) uses the metaphor of the telescope instead of the tunnel for the temporal overlapping of generations. Through processes of identification, appropriation, and intrusion, these generations slide into one another like an extendable telescope that brings what appears to be far away very close and tangible. In a "telescoping of generations" the child becomes a part of themselves in the perception of the parents through the connection of parental narcissism and identification processes. In this process, the part of their life story that the parents themselves cannot bear is deposited in the child via projective identification. The narratives that the children have to keep within themselves are not passed on by the parents through explicit stories, but as unconsciously effective messages through the way they speak. Faimberg outlines a narcissistic object relationship between parents and children. Parents inscribe themselves as they appear to the child in the transference relationship into the child's psychic reality as "inner parents." This figure of the "inner parent" structures the child's psyche through identification. The alienated, split-off part of the ego identified with the narcissistic logic of the parents is explained:

> All that deserves to be loved is me, although it comes from you, the child (When I say "the child" I am referring to the internal experience of the child and the acknowledgment of a psychical space of its own). What I acknowledge as coming from you, the child, I hate; on the other hand you will be loaded with all that I do not accept in me: you the child, will be my not-me. (ibid., pp. 106–107)

Faimberg distinguishes between the moments of appropriation and intrusion, which are fundamental to narcissistic object regulation. Narcissistic love works in the service of appropriation; narcissistic hatred fulfills the function of intrusion.

The traumatic history of the parents, which usually took place before the children were born, thus becomes their own.

From the perspective of family systems and attachment theory, **Dan Bar-On** (1998) examines the transmission mechanism of trauma and, in particular, the communication style between Shoah survivors and their children. He refers to the so-called "conspiracy of silence" (Bar-On et al. 1998). This describes the unconscious mutual avoidance of discussing the traumatic experience. Bar-On describes the communication between parents and children, which is characterized by uncertainty, using the metaphor of a double wall: "The second generation became sensitive to their parents' needs to keep silent responding with a "double wall". The parents did not tell and the children did not ask. When there was a need to make windows in the wall, as a rule, one side met with the wall of the other" (ibid., p. 326). In this way, the shared unspoken consent of avoidance is maintained. Finally, the parents' unprocessed traumatic experience leads to an ambivalent attachment to the child.

Finally, **Yael Danieli** (1998) pursues a multidimensional integrative approach. In her earlier work, she differentiated four different "adaptational styles", which represent a typification of the survival strategies of those affected and shape the children in the process of transmission: *victim style, fighter style, numb style, those who made it.* She describes the trauma of the parents as "fixity", triggered by the confrontation with a traumatic event: "The time, duration, extent and meaning of the trauma for the individual and the survival mechanisms/strategies used to adapt to it will determine the elements and degree of rupture, fragmentation and disorientation – the severity of the fixity" (Danieli et al. 2016, p. 640). In the process of adaptation, children learn specific behaviors and develop ways of coping to respond to the milieu shaped by the traumatized parent.

> In the extreme, survival strategies generalize to a way of life and become enduring *posttrauma adaptational styles.* These adaptational styles will thus shape the survivors' family life and, in turn, their children's upbringing, emotional development, identity, and beliefs about themselves, their peers, their societies and the world.... (ibid.; emphasis added)

She names the influence of the parents on the children, the aspirations of the offspring to free themselves and their parents from the trauma, as "reparative adaptational impacts": "By reparative, I want to emphasise that the childrens's main mission in life, conscious or not, is to repair the parents and themselves from the trauma" (Danieli 2019).

5.2   Practical Example: Transgenerationality in Psychotherapy

As an example, we refer to the case description of psychotherapeutic conversations with a Shoah survivor (and partly his son) reported by the psychoanalyst Kurt Grünberg (2013). Using the case vignette of "Alfred Silbermann," Grünberg demonstrates the importance of a scenic memory in the context of psychotherapeutic work with Shoah survivors and their descendants. With this approach, he focuses on the nonverbal, scenic mediation of trauma in survivor families. The manifold symptoms are primarily not present linguistically, but bodily-performatively. They are an expression of a "scenic memory".

Trying to "understand" extreme trauma is almost impossible, "because here one finds oneself in the border area of what is comprehensible to human understanding" (Grünberg and Markert 2013, p. 197). The ability to symbolize already fails in experiencing and thus inevitably in conscious remembering. The focus of scenic remembering of the Shoah therefore shifts towards bodily expressions and perceptions. The consideration of transference and counter-transference is essential here. In the encounter between survivors and other persons, the "fragmented, dissociated and unprocessable memories" (Grünberg and Markert 2013, p. 197) can break through, initiating enacting and reenacting. Children of survivors are left with hardly any possibility to escape the relational modes mediated by this.

About the case vignette: Alfred Silbermann is 85 years old when he approaches the Jewish psychotherapeutic counselling centre in Frankfurt with a request for a home visit; he is looking for help for his son Gabriel after his suicide attempt. Grünberg complies with this request, even though the treatment outside the practice, entering private rooms, should actually be considered a violation of the abstinence rule. He emphasizes that it can be beneficial to be able to include the home as a "scene" arranged by the sufferer, because there "one can grasp the aftermath of the extreme trauma in their social and spatial contexts better than anywhere else" (Grünberg 2013, p. 66). It quickly becomes clear that it is not primarily Gabriel who needs help, as he is already in psychotherapy. The trauma of his father, as well as the difficult relationship between the two that has been shaped by it, is the focus. Gabriel, who lives with his father, had jumped out of a window and survived with minor injuries. We learn about his father's life and persecution as well as his father's behaviour towards his son, which seems to be marked by contempt and hatred. The suicide attempt turns out to be an unconscious transposition in Kestenberg's sense: in a diary excerpt that Silbermann had copied for Grünberg, he recorded how the Nazis searched all the apartments, killed the younger children immediately or threw them onto a truck as if they were already dead, where those below gradually suffocated. The mother of one of these children, who lived with him in the house, threw herself out of the window in the evening and died. Gabriel tried to do the same as this dead woman, whom the father mourns to this day. Besides this level, Grünberg also considers the suicide attempt as a "completely failed separation-individuation attempt" (ibid.,: p. 69). In Grünberg's presence, Mr. Silbermann repeatedly devalues his son in an open and aggressive manner. He once inadvertently refers to the suicide attempt as a "suicide assassination" (ibid., p. 70), subliminally suspecting that this act was also directed against him. An analyst's dream becomes the key to the destructive relational dynamic: "A detective tells me that the last survivor to die in Frankfurt was killed; and that because he did not agree to the publication of his memoirs. As I claim to know many survivors, I fall under suspicion. But my suspicion falls on the son of a survivor who was in analysis with me: whether he could have killed his father?" (ibid., p. 72) In psychoanalytic perspective, Grünberg interprets this as a countertransference dream, a reaction to Silbermann in which "murderous impulses" (ibid., p. 73) he feels towards him are expressed. Grünberg understands himself at this point as identified with the son who has been repeatedly devalued by his father, whose forbidden, repressed aggressions he acts out in his place in the dream. These aggressions feel forbidden not only because of his simultaneous love for his father, but because of his father's trauma, the real history of persecution in which he was to be annihilated, which is why Gabriel does not want to fall into the role of the persecutors, does not want to reinforce his father's perceived fears of annihilation or give them cause. Grünberg tells Silbermann about this dream, whereupon the latter becomes afraid that his defences will collapse and emotions will flood him; he wants to terminate psychotherapy, but continues it (cf. ibid., p. 74).

When Gabriel has to return to the closed psychiatric ward because his depression worsens, Silbermann factually ends his psychotherapy, denies the reciprocity of the entanglements between his son and himself and destruction again dominates his actions. The mechanisms of telescoping described by Faimberg are impressively demonstrated in Gabriel and Alfred: the son is not allowed to be a person of his own, only "the father's self-object" (ibid., p. 77).

The case vignette demonstrates that the unspeakable nevertheless continuously unfolds its aggressive-destructive effect. In the case of Alfred Silbermann, this is shown on the one hand by his cynicism and aloofness, which unconsciously serves to prevent emotional closeness to people in order to protect himself from disappointment, and on the other hand in the severe depression of his son, who acts out his father's repulsed feelings of annihilation and tries to compensate with suicidal acts. The overstrained son does not understand this dilemma, only feels it in his own body, can only act. With the help of "scenic memory", however, the linguistic symbolization succeeds via the detour of the analyst's identification with him, his countertransference dream and its subsequent interpretation (cf. ibid., p. 74).

5.3   Critical Reflection

Although the issue of transgenerational transmission is gaining attention, it remains controversial at the socio-political level, especially when it comes to the recognition of financial claims or the provision of psychosocial services for the following generations. Scientific findings in the field of epigenetics are often cited in political discourse as "proof" of the reality of trauma, but this field is still new and many questions remain unanswered. It also remains to be verified how these findings will be helpful in practice.

More important seems to be the question of dealing with it on a social level – the consideration of communicative family contexts and psychotherapeutic treatment. A distinction must be made between individual mechanisms of transference and contexts in which the socio-political dimension of a historical experience of injustice plays a role. Certainly, one can also speak of a collective experience in the case of the descendants of perpetrators, but it becomes problematic when this decontextualizes verbalization of one's own experience of suffering without historical references to a common suffering.

A field of tension arises between individual psychological confrontation and the political claim of coming to terms with history. The trauma of the survivors, their descendants and those connected to the persecuted through their identity contains the experience of annihilation and stigmatization. In this context, it cannot be separated from the experience of structural political exclusion – a policy of extermination that was supported by the majority of society. Stigmatization and anti-Semitism continue to shape the political debate in post-war society to this day. The German perpetrators, on the other hand, cannot be seen as collectively traumatized in this sense. Here, the concept of emotional inheritance, introduced by Freud, is helpful. On the German side, as Jan Lohl (2010) has pointed out, emotional legacies are the desire to defend oneself as well as repressed guilt and shame that are passed on to children and grandchildren. What follows is anti-anti-Semitism, paranoid fear of Jewish revenge, the transfiguration of one's own family history and the desire for "closure". Thus, one can say: every transmission of trauma can be understood as an emotional inheritance, but not every emotional inheritance is traumatic.

Concepts of Collective Traumatization 6

The reference to concepts of collective trauma that we present (Sect. 6.1) oscillates between metaphor, diagnosis and social psychological approach. This is as an example illustrated by the socio-political reference to collective trauma in the course of the truth commissions in South Africa (Sect. 6.2). In a critical appraisal, we thus arrive at an ambivalent assessment of the scientific and practical usefulness of the concepts cited (Sect. 6.3).

6.1 Theoretical Foundations and Empirical Findings

The collective level of trauma is a scientifically contested field. In the different concepts, it is possible to show which features are considered particularly central on the basis of the leading phenomenon chosen in each case. Even if the concepts claim to be transferable to other collective phenomena, weaknesses become apparent in the concrete attempt to implement them. The concepts differ with regard to the questions of whether the trauma under consideration in each case is collective because it affects a group of victims quite abruptly or because it has been culturally collectivized, and whether this collectivization can be better explained via discursive or familial transmission.

Chosen Trauma ("Chosen Trauma") **Vamik Volkan** (2001) developed the concept of "chosen trauma". He assumes that collectives "choose" suitable historical events for their identity, which enter the collective memory as trauma.

© The Author(s), under exclusive license to Springer Fachmedien   29
Wiesbaden GmbH, part of Springer Nature 2023
P. C. Langer et al., *Trauma concepts in research and practice*, essentials,
https://doi.org/10.1007/978-3-658-40484-0_6

> Chosen trauma refers to the mental representation of an event that resulted in one group suffering severe loss at the hands of another, being made to feel helpless and victimized, and having to share a humiliating injury with each other. (Volkan 1999, p. 73)

The affected identity collective keeps the trauma narrative alive for generations and can instrumentalize it for current political purposes, as Volkan illustrates with his central example, the Yugoslavian war, which was charged with genocidal dynamics.

Kühner (2007) criticizes Volkan's approach for narrowing political events to psychological processes. Moreover, the characteristics with which he describes "chosen traumas" are formulated too generally and would inadmissibly elevate different historical events and their consequences to a common level (cf. Kühner 2007, p. 107).

Genocidal Trauma   Andreas Hamburger (2017) uses the terms "social trauma" and "genocidal trauma". His guiding phenomenon here is genocide, whereby those parts of the group, who were not direct victims but were "included," are also affected by trauma. This collective dimension of the experience of violence is reflected on a social and socio-interactive level. The violence that underlies genocidal trauma is in its intention always directed at a collective and, through the intention of the perpetrators, inscribes itself in the collective memory and the collective identity of the "victim" group, also in the following generations.

Cultural Trauma   Jeffrey Alexander (2004) has developed a decidedly cultural-sociological approach. In his concept of "cultural trauma", the concrete characteristics of the specific traumatic event are only of secondary importance. Much more important is the subsequent interpretation – the public narrative about the event – whose development depends on social power relations. The role of slavery for the collective identity of black Americans in the USA, for example, is cited as a leading phenomenon of cultural trauma. Central to this is that it is not "the collective" that makes the decision, but concretely identifiable "reflexive actors" who try to make the collective aware "that a fundamental violation has occurred", that something sacred has been attacked (Kühner 2007, p. 109). The collective is not already traumatized by the event, but must first be "convinced" in the aftermath that it has been traumatized. For Alexander, collective trauma is not something "natural," but a social construct.

Historical Trauma   The term "historical trauma" is often used to describe the collective after-effects of colonialism and slavery as a leading phenomenon. It was coined by **Maria Yellow Horse Brave Heart** in the 1980s. It focuses on the intergenerational dimension: "Historical trauma (HT) is cumulative emotional and psychological wounding, over the lifespan and across generations, emanating from massive group trauma experiences" (Brave Heart 2003, p. 7). In this regard, **Joy DeGruy** (2005) refers to "Post Traumatic Slave Syndrome" as.

> a set of behaviors, beliefs and actions associated with or, related to multi-generational trauma experienced by African Americans that include but are not limited to undiagnosed and untreated posttraumatic stress disorder (PTSD) in enslaved Africans and their descendants.

"Historical trauma" means that the event understood traumatically has a historical scale. In this sense it is close to conceptions of cultural and social as well as chosen trauma. By conceiving of historical trauma as a "public narrative", the focus is on the importance of the dominant narrative for both social reception and the mental health of those who identify with it. It should be critically noted, however, that this often entrenches specific identities. Moreover, one might ask whether the "postcolonial grief" associated with the historical narrative of suffering is truly posttraumatic. Is "trauma" an appropriate metaphor for this experience?

Symbol-Mediated Trauma   Angela Kühner (2008) proposes the concept of "symbol-mediated trauma" (p. 60) for indirectly experienced, culturally appropriated traumas that have been mediated symbolically, e.g. through the media. They inscribe themselves in a cultural representation. *9/11* can be regarded as a symbol-mediated trauma for the USA or the Western world or those who identify with it. The event was associated with a shaking of world confidence; the sense of security was lost in a statistically measurable way. Collective trauma in this sense is a multiply mediated collectivized trauma that operates through a constructed collective identity (cf. ibid.). Just as only subsequent discursive processing of what has been suffered in jointly shared (e.g. national) narratives (which may have been preceded by a collectivization of the victims by the perpetrators) collectivises it, participation in a collective identity can lead to "contagion" with its traumas. This shifts the theoretical frame of reference from psychological understandings of mental health damage to social and cultural science conceptions of cultural memory, the social unconscious, and collective identity.

6.2   Practical Example: Truth Commissions in South Africa

Let us look at an example that is often cited when talking about collective trauma and its political processing: apartheid in South Africa and the Truth and Reconciliation Commissions (TRC) institutionalized after its end. As extrajudicial investigative bodies, TRCs investigate the history of human rights violations by specific parties in the conflict.

Apartheid, centuries of racism, white military and police crimes, terrorist attacks by black resistance groups and right-wing nationalists have brought on many individual traumatic experiences of violence. "Segregation" was enshrined in law as a tool to secure white domination over blacks in the country, and was enforced with police violence. June 16, 1976 marked a bloody culmination: Black students had organized a peaceful protest against Afrikaans instead of English as the language of instruction, which was shot down by the police. Open civil war and UN sanctions followed, and the pressure on the white minority increased. In 1992 a reform programme was launched by Prime Minister de Klerk, who negotiated with jailed ANC leader Nelson Mandela. Part of the negotiations was an amnesty agreement and the establishment of the Truth Commission, which was supposed to bring the truth to light in return for amnesty for the perpetrators. In 1994, apartheid officially ended and Mandela became South Africa's first black prime minister after 30 years in prison.

Let us look at some of the events negotiated before the TRC through an insightful article by Kattermann (2012). In three vignettes, she explores dilemmas of the TRC. The first, entitled *"Public trauma processing versus subjective needs?"* shows how the logic of publicly processing collective trauma to bring all relevant information about the crime to light in an investigative way forced victims to recapitulate painful and shameful experiences, thus revealing individual vulnerabilities and reopening traumatic wounds. Kattermann interprets this as a form of replaying without working through – victimizing the victim a second time. Here, the collective runs diametrically counter to the individual processing of trauma (cf. Kattermann 2012, pp. 119–120). The second vignette *"Trauma and Reconciliation"* is about possible role confusions of perpetrators *and* victims. The affects that arise in the process described there do not want to fit the given reconciliation: The white victim, a bereaved wife of one killed, demands "punishment" for the black perpetrators despite knowledge of the amnesty provision. The descriptions of her suffering, combined with grief and aggression, lead a black member of the TRC to an affective outburst in which he pits her suffering against that of the collectively oppressed black population and morally invalidates it in light of the number of black victims. In response to the demand to bear witness to how she stood and stands by apartheid, the plaintiff is left only with the phrased reference to the mantra of reconciliation, according to which all were victims (cf. ibid., pp. 120–123). The victim in the third vignette – 'An encounter between perpetrator and victim' – is a man who sustained serious injuries in a terrorist attack on a bus carrying black people. He has filed an appeal against the amnesty application of the perpetrator, who was a member of an ultra-right Burmese group that planned and carried out the attack. There were occasional such confrontations in so-called opposition proceedings of victims against the amnesty application of the perpetrators, but they were not systematically provided for. However, insofar as the perpetrator exhibited the amnesty criterion "order of violence by a higher political structure", the emotionally presented suffering of the victim and the racist attitude of the perpetrator played no role whatsoever in the question of amnesty. It was granted to him (cf. ibid., pp. 123–125). Kattermann refers here to "the actually explosive questions of remorse, willingness to make amends, justice and morality. They are virulent in the relationship between perpetrators and victims and cannot find access through the exclusive reduction of processing to legal aspects of the crime" (ibid., p. 124).

Comprehensive amnesty was generally considered to be an unavoidable condition for the democratization process. The aim of the truth commissions was therefore not to punish perpetrators, but to make them symbolically responsible: reconciliation as a goal instead of acknowledging the insatiability of trauma. The negotiation of guilt, remorse and responsibility between the different groups on the social stage contributed to the possibility of designing a common national identity for South Africa. The discourse of reconciliation was brought into play whenever the affective charge threatened to escalate the underlying social conflicts that the very processes were intended to pacify. The talk that somehow "all were victims" makes the actors of the violence disappear. Honouring the victims can also be covertly instrumentalised for the benefit of the perpetrators: "Conversely, the discourse of reconciliation contributed to concealing the one-sided prior performance of the victims by celebrating the victims as heroes who generously forgave and at the same time were healed by the TRC. [...] Once again, it was the victims who had to put aside their concerns in the interest of collective pacification" (ibid., p. 126). The victims paid the price by having to forego not only revenge but also justice.

From a psychological point of view, the TRC could not heal traumas or bring about reconciliation between victims and perpetrators. The social conflicts present in the TRC, were partly unconsciously re-staged. The desire or the demand to be able to achieve "reconciliation" was bound to fail.

6.3   Critical Reflection

To take up the questions from the beginning once again and to subject them to a
critical answer in conclusion: Do collective traumas exist at all? Does it make sense
to use the term despite its vagueness?

Collective trauma can be seen as a framework concept for describing perceived
and felt experiences of violence, injustice and suffering by collectives, which go
beyond the individual, direct or familial experience, and for understanding their
psychosocial and socio-political dynamics. Scientifically problematic, however, is
the blurred theoretical delimitation of the phenomena subsumed under "collective
trauma": Sometimes it is about a collective constituted by a "common" experience
of violence, sometimes about a later identification with a collective thus formed. In
public discourse, reference points for such different "collective traumas" are, for
example, *9/11,* the Shoah, the genocide of the Armenians, the persecution and ex-
pulsion of the indigenous peoples of the Americas and slavery, but also war defeats
or banal events such as the defeat of a national football team, which is sometimes
framed in the media as a "national trauma".

As with individual trauma, speaking of collective trauma only makes sense if
the experience around which it revolves is one of absolute, individually experienced powerlessness.

Against the background of political instrumentalizability, it makes sense to in-
tervene as differentiating scientists in the social discourse, where a narcissistic
grievance is equated with a trauma and a competition for victimhood up to the
perpetrator-victim reversal begins. Is a "victim collective" actually traumatized, or
does it merely label itself with this loaded term to legitimize its interests? Even
more delicate is the question of whether "perpetrator collectives" can also be traumatized, possibly even by their acts themselves.

Kühner, whose work we have largely followed here, is probably right when she
notes that the concept of "collective trauma", despite all its problematics and
vagueness, should not be entirely discarded as an overarching metaphor for different cultural, social and psychological phenomena – especially when it comes to
looking at "what then remains in collectives – analogous to individual trauma –
after massive injustice" (Kühner 2008, p. 269).

Perspectives on Trauma Discourse

Violent relationships have shaped the history of humankind from its very beginning. Whether, as Steven Pinker (2011) argues, violence has declined significantly in recent centuries and we now live "in the most peaceable era in the existence of our species" is the subject of current debates (Langer 2019). However, with the globalized discourse on trauma, which is situated on different individual and collective levels, the coordinates of speaking about violence and its consequences have changed profoundly. While it was always the proverbial winners who wrote history and silenced the losers, the victims of violence are now given a powerful voice through references to trauma, which demands interpretative sovereignty over the experience, articulates the injustice suffered and is able to delegitimize the position of the perpetrators. At least the possibility of *agency* arises from once powerless weakness. The experience of the victim – as survivor and witness – is attributed a specific truth. However, it is one of the peculiarities of trauma discourse that the victim is granted this "truth", but needs others – professional witnesses – to bring it to light, to make it communicable: psychotherapists and psychiatrists in diagnosis and therapy, for example, historians through *oral history projects* or political institutions such as truth commissions. Trauma does not speak for itself.

And yet – in the logic of trauma discourse – it must be brought to language in order to break through the "conspiracy of silence". But what would it mean to oppose the imperative of speaking with the right to silence? Trauma can never be fully conceptualized anyway; it is, after all, precisely an expression of the fact that something has happened "where words cannot reach" (Keilson). In this respect, Leanh Nguyen (2011) sees the orientation towards PTSD as a reaction to an "increasingly dehumanizing and death-denying culture we live in", which is based on phantasmatic reassurance and false empowerment. Programmatically, he states:

P. C. Langer et al., *Trauma concepts in research and practice*, essentials, https://doi.org/10.1007/978-3-658-40484-0_7

"Our approach to trauma evaluation affirms that trauma can be known and measured. Our approach to treatment affirms that trauma can be repaired. Our culture of advocacy and expert testimony affirms that trauma can be easily translated, assimilated, and passed around for cultural consumption." He counters Dominik LaCapra's (2001) call to remain in a state of "empathic unsettlement" in the face of trauma.

Trauma discourse is – especially where it claims to describe supposedly individual suffering in a purely clinical way – highly political. For example, "perpetrator trauma" is certainly one of the most controversial concepts within trauma discourse, because the question arises whether perpetrators – beyond possibly corresponding symptomatology – can be "traumatized" by their deeds at all, when the core of a traumatic experience is that of complete powerlessness and becoming dehumanized. The controversy inscribed in trauma discourse demands a level of in-depth study that we have not been able to do justice to in the brevity of this introductory volume. We hope, however, that we have been able to provide intriguing suggestions with this overview, which you, as readers, can pursue – if you wish, also in a critical differentiation. Our aim is to make a plea for networking between the various professionals (as well as committed trauma victims), who can mutually enrich and advance each other with their perspectives and insights, instead of fighting for interpretive sovereignty, even if the respective understanding of trauma cannot always be brought down to a common denominator. Regardless of whether the term "trauma" is the appropriate term in every case, the point is to work together to find ways of dealing with human suffering, conflicts and (extreme) experiences of violence with an attitude of understanding.

What You Can Take Away from This *Essential*

- Trauma discourse has always been highly political. The introduction of PTSD as a clinical diagnosis indicates the latest paradigm in its history.
- The clinical conception of trauma – with PTSD as the leading diagnosis – assumes pervasive overwhelming of the individual's psychological processing abilities in confrontation with extreme events. However, psychopathologizing risks abstraction from social experiences of suffering.
- Psychosocial understandings that focus on experiences of suffering from violent social conditions emphasize the processuality of trauma in its political contexts. The conceptual psychosocial aspects remain fuzzy in many cases.
- Concepts of transgenerational transmission of trauma describe mechanisms of trauma transmission and refer to the after effects of historical injustice in different contexts. It also deals with the interconnections between socio-political reappraisal and individual methods of processing.
- Recourses to concepts of collective trauma oscillate between metaphor, diagnosis and sociopsychological claims. They do, however, provide an insightful view of the social consequences of massive injustice.

P. C. Langer et al., *Trauma concepts in research and practice*, essentials, https://doi.org/10.1007/978-3-658-40484-0

References

Alexander J (2004) Toward a theory of cultural trauma. In: Alexander J, Eyerman JR, Giesen B, Smelser NJ, Sztompka P (eds) Cultural trauma and collective identity. University of California Press, Berkeley, pp 620–639

American Psychiatric Association (2013) Diagnostic and statistical manual of mental disorders, DSM-5. American Psychiatric Association Publishing, Washington, DC

Bar-On D et al (1998) Multigenerational perspectives on coping with the Holocaust experience: an attachment perspective for understanding the developmental sequelae of trauma across generations. Int J Behav Dev 22(2):315–338

Becker D (2014) Die Erfindung des Traumas: verflochtene Geschichten. Psychosozial, Gießen

Bettelheim B (1943) Individual and mass behavior in extreme situations. J Abnorm Soc Psychol 38(4):417–452

Bettelheim B (1980) Erziehung zum Überleben. Zur Psychologie der Extremsituation. Deutsche Verlagsanstalt, Stuttgart

Bogner A, Rosenthal G (2019) KindersoldatInnen im Kontext. Universitätsverlag, Göttingen

Brave Heart MY (2003) The historical trauma response among natives and its relationship with substance abuse: a Lakota illustration. J Psychoactive Drugs 35(1):7–13

Brenssell A (2014) Traumaverstehen. In: Weber K (ed) Störungen. Argument Verlag, Hamburg, pp 123–150

Brewin CR (2005) Systematic review of screening instruments for adults at risk of PTSD. J Trauma Stress Off Publ Int Soc Trauma Stress Stud 18(1):53–62

Brewin CR (2020) Complex post-traumatic stress disorder: a new diagnosis in ICD-11. BJPsych Adv 26(3):145–152

Brunner M (2014) Trauma und Gesellschaftlicher Kontext. In: Zentralwohlfahrtstelle der Juden in Deutschland (ed) Betreuung und Belastung. Herausforderungen bei der psychosozialen Versorgung von Überlebenden der Shoah. ZWST, Frankfurt a. M., pp 8–17

Danieli Y (ed) (1998) International handbook of multigenerational legacies of trauma. Plenum Press, New York

Danieli Y (2019, 22 May) How is trauma passed on through generations? Interview with M. Armoudian. https://www.thebigq.org/2019/05/22/qa-how-is-trauma-passed-on-through-generations. Retrieved: July 18, 2020

Danieli Y, Norris FH, Engdahl B (2016) Multigenerational legacies of trauma: modeling the what and how of transmission. Am J Orthopsychiatry 86(6):639–651

DeGruy J (2005) Post traumatic slave syndrome. America's legacy of enduring injury and healing. Joy DeGruy Pub. Inc, Portland

Dreßing H (2016) Kriterien bei der Begutachtung der Posttraumatischen Belastungsstörung (PTBS). Hessisches Ärzteblatt 5:271–275

Eckhardt-Henn A, Spitzer C (2018) Dissoziative Bewusstseinsstörungen: grundlagen, Klinik, Therapie. Schattauer, Stuttgart

Elliott R et al (2021) Prevalence and predictive value of ICD-11 post-traumatic stress disorder and Complex PTSD diagnoses in children and adolescents exposed to a single-event trauma. J Child Psychol Psychiatry 62(3):270–276

Faimberg H (1988) The telescoping of generations. Contemp Psychoanal 24(1):99–118

Fassin D, Rechtman R (2009) The empire of trauma. An inquiry into the condition of victimhood. Princeton University Press, Princeton

Franklin TH et al (2010) Epigenetic transmission of the impact of early stress across generations. Biol Psychiatry 68:408–415

Gerdau I, Kizilhan JI, Noll-Hussong M (2017) Posttraumatic stress disorder and related disorders among female Yazidi refugees following Islamic state of Iraq and Syria attacks—a case series and mini-review. Front Psych 8:282

GIZ (2019) Guiding framework for mental health and psychosocial support (MHPSS) in Development Cooperation. https://www.giz.de/en/downloads/giz2018-en-guiding-framework-MHPSS.pdf. Retrieved: July 18, 2020

Grünberg K (2013) Szenisches Erinnern der Shoah. "Das abenteuerliche Leben des Alfred Silbermann". In: Grillmeyer S (ed) Juden in Mitteleuropa. Echter, Würzburg, pp 58–67. http://www.injoest.ac.at/files/jme_2013.pdf. Retrieved: July 11, 2020

Grünberg K, Markert F (2013) Todesmarsch und Grabeswanderung. Szenisches Erinnern der Shoah. Psyche 76:1071–1099

Hamburger A (2017) Genocidal trauma. In: Laub D, Hamburger A (eds) Psychoanalysis and Holocaust testimony: unwanted memories of social trauma. Routledge, London, pp 66–91

Herzog D (2017) Cold war Freud: psychoanalysis in an age of catastrophes. Cambridge University Press, Cambridge

Hoge CW, Castro CA, Messer SC, McGurk D, Cotting DI, Koffman RL (2004) Combat duty in Iraq and Afghanistan, mental health problems, and barriers to care. N Engl J Med 351(1):13–22

Hyland P, Shevlin M, McNally S, Murphy J, Hansen M, Elklit A (2016) Exploring differences between the ICD-11 and DSM-5 models of PTSD: does it matter which model is used? J Anxiety Disord 37:48–53

Jowett S, Karatzias T, Shevlin M, Albert I (2020) Differentiating symptom profiles of ICD-11 PTSD, complex PTSD, and borderline personality disorder: a latent class analysis in a multiply traumatized sample. Pers Disord Theory Res Treatment 11(1):36–45

Kapfhammer H-P (2018) Trauma und Traumafolgestörungen. https://oegpb.at/2018/05/28/trauma-und-trauma-folgestoerungen. Retrieved: July, 10 2020

Kattermann V (2012) Vertrauen in die Mitwelt. Trauma, Schuld und Versöhnung am Beispiel der südafrikanischen Warheits-und Versöhnungskommission. In: Karger A (ed) Vergessen, Vergelten, Vergeben, Versöhnen? Weiterleben mit dem Trauma. Psychoanalytische Blätter, vol 30. Vandenhoeck & Ruprecht, Göttingen

Keilson H, Sarphatie HR (1992) Sequential traumatization in children: a clinical and statistical follow-up study on the fate of the Jewish war orphans in the Netherlands. Magnes Press, Jerusalem

Kestenberg JS (1989) Neue Gedanken zur Transposition. Klinische, therapeutische und entwicklungsbedingte Betrachtungen. Jb Psychoanal 24:163–189

Keupp H, Straus F, Mosser P, Gmür W, Hackenschmied G (2016) Sexueller Missbrauch und Misshandlungen in der Benediktinerabtei Ettal: ein Beitrag zur wissenschaftlichen Aufarbeitung. Springer, Wiesbaden

Kuch K, Cox BJ (1992) Symptoms of PTSD in 124 survivors of the Holocaust. Am J Psychiatry 149(3):337–340

Kühner A (2007) Kollektive Traumata. Konzepte, Argumente, Perspektiven. Psychosozial, Gießen

Kühner A (2008) Trauma und kollektives Gedächtnis. Psychosozial, Gießen

LaCapra D (2001) Writing trauma, writing history. Johns Hopkins University Press, Baltimore

Langer PC (2013) Wenn's nicht näher als 30 Meter neben mir knallt, dann nehmen wir es nicht mehr persönlich. Freie Assoziation 16(2):69–86

Langer PC (2019) Sozial- als Friedenspsychologie denken. In: Kirchhoff C, Kühn T, Langer PC, Lanwerd S, Schumann F (eds) Psychoanalytisch denken. Psychosozial, Gießen

Langer PC (2020) Keine Zukunft. Nirgends. Zu Erfahrungen ehemaliger Kindersoldaten des "Islamischen Staates" im Nordirak. In: Tolle P (ed) Von vernünftigen und unvernünftigen Zuständen. Psychosozial, Gießen, pp 109–144

Langer PC, Ahmad A-N (2019) Psychosocial needs of former ISIS child soldiers in northern Iraq. IPU, Berlin. https://www.ipu-berlin.de/fileadmin/downloads/forschung/isis-report.pdf. Retrieved: July, 18 2020

Langer PC, Brehm A (2020) Social trauma: a social psychological perspective. In: Hamburger A et al (eds) Interdisciplinary handbook of social trauma. Springer, Heidelberg, pp 219–233

Laub D (2005) From speechlessness to narrative: the cases of Holocaust historians and of psychiatrically hospitalized survivors. Lit Med 24(2):253–265

Lehmacher ATK (2013) Trauma-Konzepte im historischen Wandel: Ein Beitrag zur Rezeptionsgeschichte der Posttraumatic-Stress Disorder in Deutschland (1980–1991). Dissertation at the Rheinische Friedrich-Wilhelms-Universität Bonn

Lohl J (2010) Gefühlserbschaft und Rechtsextremismus, Eine sozialpsychologische Studie zur Generationengeschichte des Nationalsozialismus. Psychosozial, Gießen

Maercker A (2013) Psychologische Modelle. In: Maercker A (ed) Posttraumatische Belastungsstörungen, 4th edn. Springer, Berlin, pp 35–54

Miller KE, Rasmussen A (2010) War exposure, daily stressors, and mental health in conflict and post-conflict settings: bridging the divide between trauma-focused and psychosocial frameworks. Soc Sci Med 70:7–16

Nguyen L (2011) The ethics of trauma: re-traumatization in society's approach to the traumatized subject. Int J Group Psychother 61(1):26–47

Pinker S (2011) The better angels of our nature: The decline of violence in history and its causes. Penguin, New York

Pole N, Best SR, Metzler T, Marmar CR (2005) Why are Hispanics at greater risk for PTSD? Cultur Divers Ethnic Minor Psychol 11(2):144–161

Regier DA, Narrow WE, Clarke DE, Kraemer HC, Kuramoto SJ, Kuhl EA, Kupfer DJ (2013) DSM-5 field trials in the United States and Canada, Part II: test-retest reliability of selected categorical diagnoses. Am J Psychiatry 170(1):59–70

Repnik F (2018) Gewalt, Trauma und Religion in Kolumbien. Nomos, Baden-Baden

Ronel J (2020) Ein Ort zum Reden, ein Ort zum Schweigen. Das Münchener "Café Zelig" der letzten Überlebenden der Shoah im Kontext der deutschen Mehrheitsgesellschaft. Psychosozial 43(3):38–50

Roth Tania L (2014) How traumatic experiences leave their signature on the genome: an overview of epigenetic pathways in PTSD. Front Psych 5:93

Schmiedebach HP (2019) Geschichte der Psychotraumatologie. In: Maercker A (ed) Traumafolgestörungen, 4th edn. Springer, Berlin, pp 3–12

Schroer-Hippel M, Cohrs JC, Vollhardt JR (2018) Sozialpsychologische Friedens-und Konfliktforschung. In: Decker O (ed) Sozialpsychologie und Sozialtheorie. Springer, Wiesbaden, pp 97–109

Schuy K et al (2019) "Treffer im Kopf" – Stigma psychischer Erkrankungen als Einflussfaktor auf die Inanspruchnahme von Hilfsangeboten durch VeteranInnen der Bundeswehr. Das Gesundheitswesen 81(8–9):e146–e153

Seiffert A, Langer PC, Pietsch C (eds) (2011) Der Einsatz der Bundeswehr in Afghanistan: sozial-und politikwissenschaftliche Perspektiven. Springer, Wiesbaden

Shorter E (1993) From paralysis to fatigue: a history of psychosomatic illness in the modern era. Free Press, New York

Streeck-Fischer A (2019) Borderland and borderline: understanding and treating adolescent migrants in crisis. Adolesc Psychiatry 9(3):185–193

Traicu A, Joober R (2017) The value of a skeptical approach to neurosciences in psychiatric training and practice. J Psychiatry Neurosci 42(6):363

Trappler B, Braunstein JW, Moskowitz G, Friedman S (2002) Holocaust survivors in a primary care setting: Fifty years later. Psychol Rep 91(2):545–552

Volkan VD (1999) Das Versagen der Diplomatie. Zur Psychoanalyse nationaler, ethnischer und religiöser Konflikte. Psychosozial, Gießen

Volkan VD (2001) Transgenerational transmissions and chosen traumas: an aspect of large-group identity. Group Analysis 34(1):79–97

Weltgesundheitsorganisation (WHO) (1994) Internationale statistische Klassifikation der Krankheiten und verwandter Gesundheitsprobleme Störungen: ICD–10, Bd 10. Springer, Berlin

Wittchen HU (2012) Traumatische Ereignisse und posttraumatische Belastungsst.rungen bei im Ausland eingesetzten Soldaten: wie hoch ist die Dunkelziffer? Dtsch Arztebl Int 109(35–36):559–568

Wizelman L (2009) Wenn der Krieg nicht endet: Schicksale von traumatisierten Soldaten und ihren Angehörigen. Psychiatrie Verlag, Bonn

Yehuda R et al (2015) Holocaust exposure induced intergenerational effects on FKBP5 methylation. Biol Psychiatry 80(5):372–380

Young A (1995) The harmony of illusions: inventing post-traumatic stress disorder. Princeton University Press, Princeton

Printed by Printforce, the Netherlands